I0449358

Simple Joy Daily
by Armando Heredia

I started doing these illustrations and focusing on joy while working through grief. It has been a great way to help me regain balance and focus.

I am continuing the journey daily and posting on Instagram at @simplejoy.daily and on my blog www.simplejoydaily.artblog.

Join me on a *Sixty Day Challenge* of finding joy in the simple things.

Add your own sketches, write down what brings you joy, paste a photo or attach an object. Don't worry about doing a certain thing, just do what gives voice to your joy. Take a pic of your joy statement and post it. #simplejoychallenge

For my son, Jon. Thank you for encouraging me to make this book.

A hot cup of coffee on a cool crisp morning brings me joy.

What brought *you* joy today?

Draw, doodle, sketch, paste, or whatever you'd like to express something that brought you joy today.

Take a pic and hashtag it #simplejoychallenge

Several years ago my wife and I visited Dead Horse Ranch in Arizona. We stood on the quietest trail, and listened to the leaves as they bumped and scratched tree branches while they fell. This cherished memory brings me joy.

What brought *you* joy today?

Draw, doodle, sketch, paste, or whatever you'd like to express something that brought you joy today.

Take a pic and hashtag it #simplejoychallenge

Spent the night in a little log cabin in the woods of northern Arizona with one of my sons.
This brings me joy.

What brought *you* joy today?

Draw, doodle, sketch, paste, or whatever you'd like to express something that brought you joy today.

Take a pic and hashtag it #simplejoychallenge

A little yellow bird landed in a branch right above our camp at Dead Horse Ranch, and started singing. My son spotted it first. This brings me joy.

What brought *you* joy today?

Draw, doodle, sketch, paste, or whatever you'd like to express something that brought you joy today.

Every day when I get home, the first few minutes are spent howling with my little dog, Jack. This brings me joy.

What brought *you* joy today?

Draw, doodle, sketch, paste, or whatever you'd like to express something that brought you joy today.

Take a pic and hashtag it #simplejoychallenge

A group of friends sat across the room this morning, drinking coffee, laughing and enjoying each other's company. This brings me joy.

What brought *you* joy today?

Draw, doodle, sketch, paste, or whatever you'd like to express something that brought you joy today.

The weather is perfect, so I can drive with the windows down and the classic rock station full blast on the radio. This brings me joy.

What brought *you* joy today?

Draw, doodle, sketch, paste, or whatever you'd like to express something that brought you joy today.

Almost every morning I have an opportunity to take a short walk in a park. Sunshine, birds, mountains in the distance. This brings me joy.

What brought *you* joy today?

Draw, doodle, sketch, paste, or whatever you'd like to express something that brought you joy today.

Yesterday I stood on the landing at the bottom of our stairs and spent time looking at photos of my kids through the years. This brings me joy.

What brought *you* joy today?

Draw, doodle, sketch, paste, or whatever you'd like to express something that brought you joy today.

Take a pic and hashtag it #simplejoychallenge

We recently rediscovered a childhood treat, a tiny shortbread cookie topped with four coconut and strawberry marshmallow. This brings me joy.

What brought *you* joy today?

Draw, doodle, sketch, paste, or whatever you'd like to express something that brought you joy today.

Take a pic and hashtag it #simplejoychallenge

There is a window that faces east at the coffee shop where I spend my morning creative time. Looking out into the sunrise brings me joy.

What brought *you* joy today?

Draw, doodle, sketch, paste, or whatever you'd like to express something that brought you joy today.

Take a pic and hashtag it #simplejoychallenge

We're in that wonderful season in Arizona, where the windows are open in the evenings and mornings. Cool air, birds singing, kids laughing.
This brings me joy.

What brought *you* joy today?

Draw, doodle, sketch, paste, or whatever you'd like to express something that brought you joy today.

Take a pic and hashtag it #simplejoychallenge

Last night my wife baked a cake and one of my sons made homemade frosting.
This brings me joy.

What brought *you* joy today?

Draw, doodle, sketch, paste, or whatever you'd like to express something that brought you joy today.

Take a pic and hashtag it #simplejoychallenge

I got to spend a couple of evenings with my oldest brother. We don't get to see each other often, because we live so far apart. This brings me joy.

What brought *you* joy today?

Draw, doodle, sketch, paste, or whatever you'd like to express something that brought you joy today.

Take a pic and hashtag it #simplejoychallenge

I got to make omelettes for my family Sunday morning. We drank Hikona Coffee that my brother and sister-in-law brought us from Hawaii.
This brings me joy.

What brought *you* today?

Draw, doodle, sketch, paste, or whatever you'd like to express something that brought you joy today.

Take a pic and hashtag it #simplejoychallenge

I had a close encounter with a roadrunner yesterday! This brings me joy.

What brought *you* joy today?

Draw, doodle, sketch, paste, or whatever you'd like to express something that brought you joy today.

Take a pic and hashtag it #simplejoychallenge

Yesterday a dear friend sent me a song he wrote and produced that has a lot of meaning to him. I stopped and listened to it at work. This brings me joy.

What brought *you* joy today?

Draw, doodle, sketch, paste, or whatever you'd like to express something that brought you joy today.

Take a pic and hashtag it #simplejoychallenge

Yesterday one of my best friends texted me that they had reached three months sobriety, and they were so happy.
This brings me joy!

What brought *you* joy today?

Draw, doodle, sketch, paste, or whatever you'd like to express something that brought you joy today.

Take a pic and hashtag it #simplejoychallenge

I cried watching Clean with Passion for Now on Netflix. There's a scene where a man has a panic attack in an airport and his friend uses an umbrella to create a safe space for him right in the midst of everything. This brings me joy.

What brought *you* joy today?

Draw, doodle, sketch, paste, or whatever you'd like to express something that brought you joy today.

Take a pic and hashtag it #simplejoychallenge

I realized that my sons have grown up to be my three closest friends. This brings me joy.

What brought *you* joy today?

Draw, doodle, sketch, paste, or whatever you'd like to express something that brought you joy today.

Take a pic and hashtag it #simplejoychallenge

Woke up to a beautiful cloudy day. This brings me joy.

What brought *you* joy today?

Draw, doodle, sketch, paste, or whatever you'd like to express something that brought you joy today.

Take a pic and hashtag it #simplejoychallenge

My newly married son had an unexpected day off and came and had lunch with us at Cracker Barrel on Sunday.
This brings me joy.

What brought **you** today?

Draw, doodle, sketch, paste, or whatever you'd like to express something that brought you joy today.

Take a pic and hashtag it #simplejoychallenge

We had the opportunity to sit and listen to my youngest son's plans and dreams last night.
This brings me joy!

What brought *you* joy today?

Draw, doodle, sketch, paste, or whatever you'd like to express something that brought you joy today.

Take a pic and hashtag it #simplejoychallenge

Picked up my son to come and stay at home for a few days. Spent the drive home singing, talking and laughing. This brings me joy.

What brought *you* joy today?

Draw, doodle, sketch, paste, or whatever you'd like to express something that brought you joy today.

Take a pic and hashtag it #simplejoychallenge

I had an amazing bowl of ramen last night with Spam and sun dried tomatoes.
This brings me joy.

What brought *you* joy today?

Draw, doodle, sketch, paste, or whatever you'd like to express something that brought you joy today.

Take a pic and hashtag it #simplejoychallenge

My wife and I stumbled on a great little food truck that sells elotes! This is our new Saturday tradition.
This brings me joy!

What brought *you* joy today?

Draw, doodle, sketch, paste, or whatever you'd like to express something that brought you joy today.

Take a pic and hashtag it #simplejoychallenge

Stopped by a farmer's market in Verrado and got to listen to an 86 year old artist talk about his life and work. This brings me joy.

What brought *you* joy today?

Draw, doodle, sketch, paste, or whatever you'd like to express something that brought you joy today.

Had a bowl of cereal for dinner last night. There are not many things that bring joy like a bowl of Cinnamon Life Cereal.

What brought *you* today?

Draw, doodle, sketch, paste, or whatever you'd like to express something that brought you joy today.

One of my friends that I haven't seen in years, and who has moved back to his home country, tagged me in a post about being friends for 13 years on FB.
This brings me joy.

What brought *you* joy today?

Draw, doodle, sketch, paste, or whatever you'd like to express something that brought you joy today.

Had a lovely spontaneous dinner at Whataburger with my wife, two sons and daughter in law, and then went for a beautiful sunset drive up into Verrado with my wife.
This brings me joy.

What brought *you* joy today?

Draw, doodle, sketch, paste, or whatever you'd like to express something that brought you joy today.

Take a pic and hashtag it #simplejoychallenge

There are a couple of elder gentlemen who I see regularly at the park where I walk in the morning. One times the other as he flies his little plane as fast as he can in a circle around them. This brings me joy.

What brought *you* joy today?

Draw, doodle, sketch, paste, or whatever you'd like to express something that brought you joy today.

This morning, my wife and I parked in the shade behind her work in a big concrete and asphalt retail development. The water run off area, with its landscaping and trees is home to a family of cottontail. This brings me joy.

What brought *you* joy today?

Draw, doodle, sketch, paste, or whatever you'd like to express something that brought you joy today.

Take a pic and hashtag it #simplejoychallenge

Yesterday I fired up the grill and made barbecue for my family. This brings me joy.

What brought *you* joy today?

Draw, doodle, sketch, paste, or whatever you'd like to express something that brought you joy today.

Take a pic and hashtag it #simplejoychallenge

All of my boys were home last night. I love just watching them interact as adults. This brings me joy.

What brought *you* joy today?

Draw, doodle, sketch, paste, or whatever you'd like to express something that brought you joy today.

Take a pic and hashtag it #simplejoychallenge

My wife made peach cobbler! A couple of scoops of vanilla bean ice cream and perfect bliss. This brings me joy.

What brought *you* joy today?

Draw, doodle, sketch, paste, or whatever you'd like to express something that brought you joy today.

Take a pic and hashtag it #simplejoychallenge

Friday morning, sitting by a window in the sunshine having an orange scone and light roast coffee at Panera Bread. This brings me joy.

What brought *you* joy today?

Draw, doodle, sketch, paste, or whatever you'd like to express something that brought you joy today.

Take a pic and hashtag it #simplejoychallenge

Ordered that cranberry orange muffin in the display case this morning at Panera.
This brings me joy.

What brought *you* today?

Draw, doodle, sketch, paste, or whatever you'd like to express something that brought you joy today.

Take a pic and hashtag it #simplejoychallenge

My wife and I ate at one of our favorite Mexican food restaurants this weekend. Good food and good company.
This brings me joy.

What brought *you* joy today?

Draw, doodle, sketch, paste, or whatever you'd like to express something that brought you joy today.

Spent some time with other entrepreneurs at the Monday Meetup in Buckeye, AZ, learning about business.
This brings me joy.

What brought *you* joy today?

Draw, doodle, sketch, paste, or whatever you'd like to express something that brought you joy today.

My son texted me yesterday and was excited to have helped someone install and set up their online streaming gear. I love seeing my kids doing what they love. This brings me joy!

What brought *you* joy today?

Draw, doodle, sketch, paste, or whatever you'd like to express something that brought you joy today.

Take a pic and hashtag it #simplejoychallenge

I was at a restaurant waiting for a work meeting. I listened to four older ladies discuss life. This brings me joy.

What brought **you** joy today?

Draw, doodle, sketch, paste, or whatever you'd like to express something that brought you joy today.

Fajitas tonight! My wife prepped everything and the chicken is marinating. This brings me joy!

What brought *you* joy today?

Draw, doodle, sketch, paste, or whatever you'd like to express something that brought you joy today.

Just witnessed two friends greet each other with genuine happiness and excitement.
This brings me joy.

What brought *you* joy today?

Draw, doodle, sketch, paste, or whatever you'd like to express something that brought you joy today.

We made chipotle chicken salad sandwiches this weekend. Chipotle aioli, black grapes, red onion, tomato, celery, shredded chicken.
This brings me joy.

What brought *you* joy today?

Draw, doodle, sketch, paste, or whatever you'd like to express something that brought you joy today.

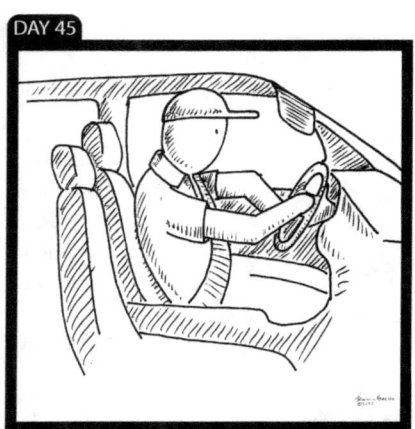

Had the opportunity to have a great conversation with one of my sons yesterday. We spent half an hour talking about his great ideas and creativity.
This brings me joy!

What brought *you* joy today?

Draw, doodle, sketch, paste, or whatever you'd like to express something that brought you joy today.

Yesterday I sat and tried to think of something new that brings me joy. I couldn't think of one thing. So, I thought back on all of the other things that have brought me joy, and that brought me joy, too.

What brought *you* joy today?

Draw, doodle, sketch, paste, or whatever you'd like to express something that brought you joy today.

My wife and I got gorditas and watermelon aguas frescas from a food truck this weekend! This brings me joy!

What brought *you* joy today?

Draw, doodle, sketch, paste, or whatever you'd like to express something that brought you joy today.

Take a pic and hashtag it #simplejoychallenge

My son picked me up for lunch yesterday. We went to Two Hands in Avondale, AZ and had some amazing corn dogs and kimchi fries. This brings me joy.

What brought *you* joy today?

Draw, doodle, sketch, paste, or whatever you'd like to express something that brought you joy today.

*Had a wonderful conversation with my brother last night.
This brings me joy!*

What brought *you* joy today?

Draw, doodle, sketch, paste, or whatever you'd like to express something that brought you joy today.

Take a pic and hashtag it #simplejoychallenge

My son found a scruffy little dog near his apartment. Of course he took it home, is caring for it and is trying to find its home. He has a big heart, and that brings me joy.

What brought *you* joy today?

Draw, doodle, sketch, paste, or whatever you'd like to express something that brought you joy today.

Sat and watched a little bird this morning. It was kicking stuff around. I'm not sure if it was trying to attract attention or looking for food under the fallen desert flower petals.
This brings me joy.

What brought *you* joy today?

Draw, doodle, sketch, paste, or whatever you'd like to express something that brought you joy today.

Take a pic and hashtag it #simplejoychallenge

We bought my wife a VCR for Mother's Day and spent part of the morning watching recordings of our boys from over twenty years ago. It brought her joy, and this brings me joy.

What brought *you* joy today?

Draw, doodle, sketch, paste, or whatever you'd like to express something that brought you joy today.

Take a pic and hashtag it #simplejoychallenge

My sons took their mom to dinner at Cheddar's Scratch Kitchen to celebrate her for Mother's Day. This brings me joy.

What brought *you* joy today?

Draw, doodle, sketch, paste, or whatever you'd like to express something that brought you joy today.

Take a pic and hashtag it #simplejoychallenge

Spent the evening doing a color mock-up for an upcoming painting. My son liked it so much he bought the mock-up, and wouldn't let me give it to him for free. He's an art patron.
This brings me joy.

What brought *you* joy today?

Draw, doodle, sketch, paste, or whatever you'd like to express something that brought you joy today.

My wife made creamy tacos last night. Stacks of soft corn tortillas in a creamy sauce, with a fried egg on top, covered with cheese, lettuce, tomatoes, and sour cream, plus homemade salsa. This brings me joy!

What brought *you* joy today?

Draw, doodle, sketch, paste, or whatever you'd like to express something that brought you joy today.

Take a pic and hashtag it #simplejoychallenge

Had an awesome birthday steak dinner at Texas Roadhouse. I turned fifty and spent most of the evening telling my family "glory days" stories like an old man.
This brings me joy.

What brought *you* joy today?

Draw, doodle, sketch, paste, or whatever you'd like to express something that brought you joy today.

Take a pic and hashtag it #simplejoychallenge

A street vendor came through our neighborhood yesterday. We got elotes and sno-cones.
This brings me joy.

What brought *you* joy today?

Draw, doodle, sketch, paste, or whatever you'd like to express something that brought you joy today.

Take a pic and hashtag it #simplejoychallenge

*Got to spend my
creative time this
morning with my
eldest son.
This brings me joy!*

What brought *you* joy today?

Draw, doodle, sketch, paste, or whatever you'd like to express something that brought you joy today.

Take a pic and hashtag it #simplejoychallenge

Got to work on a new painting over the last few days. This brings me joy.

What brought *you* joy today?

Draw, doodle, sketch, paste, or whatever you'd like to express something that brought you joy today.

Take a pic and hashtag it #simplejoychallenge

My wife and I had the best chicken teriyaki and California rolls from Chef Ben's in Goodyear. We watched the 1985 version of Anne of Green Gables on VHS.
This brings me joy!

What brought *you* joy today?

Draw, doodle, sketch, paste, or whatever you'd like to express something that brought you joy today.

Take a pic and hashtag it #simplejoychallenge